A PEARL A DAY

WITH FATHER POPS

WISE SAYINGS FOR LIVING WELL

Notes Edited By

LAWRENCE M. VENTLINE, D.MIN., PH.D.

ISBN: 1-883520-16-9
LIBRARY OF CONGRESS CATALOG NO.: 98-075729
© Copyright, 1998, Lawrence M. Ventline

Jeremiah Press, Inc.
Boca Raton, Florida

PRAYER FOR ACCEPTANCE

With full awareness that the only thing I can give You
Lord is my willingness to accept, I return unto Thee
all that I am and have, committing heart, mind and
soul to Thy infinite power and grace. Free me from
the prison of self; the illusion of independence; and,
the chains of sin. Make me an instrument of your will
and a humble apostle of your love. Now and forever.
Amen.

FOREWORD
Frederick J. Klettner
Pastor of St. Clare of Assissi Parish
Farmington Hills, Michigan

Father Edward David Popielarz came from a family of clothiers. "Fr. Pops", as he was affectionately called, knew his "stuff by golly" when it came to fine "threads". And, in his work as a Catholic priest, he could weave wonderful threads or patterns of recognition out of the deep insights he had into the structures of our daily living.

As a young priest, I was evicted from my parish (for attacking authority rightly or wrongly-who cares?) and sent to the Shrine Parish of St. Joseph, Pontiac, Michigan from which I would minister as a hospital chaplain, and in which I would encounter the new pastor, Fr. Popielarz. I was angry, upset, resentful, and I didn't want to be there. Also, in the seminary and the early days of my priesthood, I went through a painful psychological-spiritual sickness called scrupulosity in which you think everything you do is a serious sin. So, I was a good candidate for Pop's Acceptance Class, which he had started some years earlier to share his renewal of life after the depths of alcoholism.

Again and again, Pops would say to me: "Whatever our situation, we only have one problem that we all share-FEAR!" Showing up for Class in Acceptance became a staple in my life, and, at first, I was confused by it and yet drawn to it at the same time. Gradually, as I stayed the course, my life began to shift while the power of my demons receded. Over time, as I practiced the principles and used the wisdom of the class in my daily affairs, I soon began to realize their value.

3

After having been involved with the class for some time, one day I found myself at a session of the Pontiac City Commission, which was attempting to deal with the stormy issued of bussing school children for the purpose of racial integration. At the meeting I stood up to speak in a crowd of upset, angry, hostile citizens-to put it mildly. Yet, after my little, naïve presentation on Acceptance, the room, to my great surprise, and relief, grew very quiet-spiritually-still even-and the tension left. People felt squeamish about their intolerance and guilty about the enjoyment they previously had over hating one another. It was then that I saw Pop's sense of things could have impact even beyond a small group setting and be taken into the larger social arena. Truly, an astounding moment!

When you, the reader, go through the pages of Fr. Lawrence Ventline's **A Pearl A Day** I'm sure you will be struck by the richness of thought that lies before you. However, what powerfully brings this feast of insight to life is the celebration of it in a live assemblage of seeking souls. For, this is knowledge of the Spirit and the Spirit works in the realm of the interpersonal.

Fr. Pop's purpose in life, as I saw it, was to take his experience, insights and wisdom garnered as a professor in the seminary, a priest in pastoral life and a member of Alcoholics Anonymous and share it with those, who simply struggled with their everyday existence. He felt that everyone could benefit from Acceptance even though their problems may not be as dramatic as those suffered by the chemically dependent.

Fr. Ventline has done a wonderful service for all those who seek the healing balm of God's wisdom, by sharing and organizing the work of Fr. Pop's, the Ambassador of Acceptance. Acceptance, for Fr. Popielarz, was always the place to start in dealing with the problems coming from our inner turmoil. "Accept the 'mess' you're in, my little Fredzue (Freddie)," he would say to me as we sailed forth over waves of lively conversation stimulated by his far-reaching, religious imagination. Edward David Popielarz was a master in life, and he created the space for me to become one also.

As I begin my twentieth year of moderating an Acceptance Class, I am ever grateful for being sent many years ago, against my will, to dwell in the wonderful world of Fr. Pops.

A PEARL A DAY:
WISE SAYINGS FOR LIVING WELL

INTRODUCTION

Remembering "Father Pops"
by Lawrence M. Ventline

After football practice in high school, I would trek a couple of miles home near Detroit's city airport before promptly reporting for work each evening at the parish rectory to answer the door and the telephone of a busy Catholic church.

Little did I realize the impact that Father Edward Popielarz-one of the four assistant pastors- would have on me. Affectionately known as "Father Pops"—his hard-to-pronounce Polish last name means "garbage man"—I remember him most for what was dubbed as "a class in acceptance."

Each Wednesday night, about a hundred people would crowd the cracker-box gym of St. Thomas the Apostle Church on Detroit's East Side, not far from downtown. The "mix" of ages, colors, and creeds—of what an outsider would call a "mixed up" group—crowded around Father Pops, who provided each participant with a perfectly typed sheet of mental-health notes that were numbered from 1 through 10 or more.

So who was this wonderful man, a recovering alcoholic pastor, whose anniversary of passing from this life to the next is marked every December by the thousands of people who came to him for solace?

Born in Saginaw, Michigan, the youngest of eight children, Edward Popielarz grew up in Hamtramck, the then largely Polish enclave that was surrounded by Detroit. He attended high school and college at the Orchard Lake Schools—a Polish seminary where Father Pops spent half of his priestly career in various teaching and administrative posts. In the second half, he served as a parish priest, including an assignment at a poor Pontiac parish where he continued his acceptance classes and launched a free health clinic in 1974.

"When you are ailing, I think you are closer to God than at any other time," Father Pops said when a few parishioners were upset that the church sacristy was used as the clinic's examination room.

Educated at the Catholic University in Washington D.C., he relished telling the story of someone sneaking onto the church grounds to paint black faces on all the white marble statues of Mary and Jesus. During the next night, someone else would paint them all white again. "Gold is a neutral color that shines with love," Father Pops told me, explaining how he personally painted each statue gold.

What keeps people from loving is a fear complex, Father Pops taught in his acceptance classes. "Fear makes people want to control people," he said, as he helped countless people cut through such fears as losing one's health, freedom, material security and dependent relationships.

Fond of theologian Paul Tillich, Father Pops defined acceptance as "recognizing one's problem and seeking the answer in one's self," and immediately he would turn to Tillich's *The Shaking of the Foundations:*

> Sometimes at the moment (of despair) a
> wave of light breaks into your darkness, and it is
> as though a voice were saying: "You are accepted.
> You are accepted, accepted by that which is greater
> than you and the name of which you do not know.

Do not ask for the name now; perhaps you will find it later. Do not try to do anything now; perhaps later you will do much. Do not seek for anything, do not intend anything. Simply accept the fact that you are accepted." If that happens to us, we experience grace. After such an experience, everything is transformed. In that moment, grace conquers sin, and reconciliation bridges the gulf of estrangement.

According to Father Pops, the movement from fear to acceptance involves five steps:

1. Make a decision to accept myself and the mess I'm in. Accept the problem.
2. Make contact with people so that I can break contact with the problem. When I'm attuned to others, my problems are not thought about.
3. By being in contact with people who have my problem, I understand how it came about.
4. By making the acquaintance of people with similar problems, and relating to "the other," I can become loving.
5. Develop empathy, which is the skill that helps me to be more accepting of another's position without becoming emotionally involved.

He believed that acceptance could also be defined as "recognizing one's problem and seeking the answer in oneself, while in communion with others." There are four steps to acceptance: know it, admit it, accept it and live it. To accept self is to sort of jump out of my skin and look at myself from the sidelines. I don't always like what I see. I see attitudes that look mean; these I can change if I try, but I also see limitations that cannot be changed, such as my intellectual and emotional endowments. Nor can I wipe out my background nor my physical makeup. Why pine away in wanting what is not? I accept myself. It is humbling, but it is also quieting.

To accept is to become comfortable with what I cannot change, by disciplining self, by changing my outlook. By getting to know myself, by accepting myself. I eliminate fear, thus making it possible to see the problem better.

In his truthful disposition, Father Pops was quick to admit that if there ever was a bad sinner, he or she couldn't be any worse than he was. He concluded that if our attitude toward people—regardless of race, creed or color—is right, then we will be ready to get the message that God wants to convey to us, a message that has also been made manifest through the civil disturbances our cities have suffered: "If our attitude is right, then willingly we do the job that justice demands be done, so that we will not need to be reminded again by God by way of another social tragedy."

For me, Father Pops was fresh air on fear, on fairness, on his ability to accept the old and the new. "The Church should never reject the old ways but only accept new ways," he would teach.

Once when I visited his acceptance class, a sign in front of the Pontiac church advertised: "We celebrate Masses, retreats, novenas, pilgrimages, festivals, vigils, "the living Rosary," devotions, lectures, classes, buffets, excursions, recitals and blessings."

"The man is comfortable with the traditional and the contemporary," I thought to myself. "What a reconciler!" What a gift he possessed!

Always seeing spirituality as the unique thirst of humans, Father Pops seemed to know decades ago that addictions today are ontological and anthropological issues that cannot be resolved with psychology alone. A prayer seems to best sum up the eight beatitudes as expressed in the acceptance classes:

Holy God, we ask you:

Make us personable. We will value "being" higher than "having." *Blessed are the poor in spirit for theirs is the kingdom of heaven.*

Make us active. We will accept each cross sent our way and make of each a heaven-sent stimulant to propel us onto action, never before imagined. *Blessed are they who mourn, for they shall be comforted.*

Make us trainable. We will stop manipulating self and others. Humbly we will find our rightful place among others. Only then will we be ready to learn and to do. *Blessed are the meek, for they shall possess the earth.*

Make us practical. We will shun perfectionism. With flexibility we will seek and develop techniques that will bring about change in our own lives and in others. *Blessed are they that hunger and thirst for justice, for they shall be satisfied*

Make us compassionate. We will show mercy, always aware that we are incomplete, and that every one of us can slip away from great ideals, regress and deteriorate. *Blessed are the merciful for they shall obtain mercy.*

Make us single-minded. We will love enduringly and devotedly, knowing that the only way to be loved is to love. *Blessed are the pure of heart, for they shall see God.*

Make us imaginative. We will always resort to imagination, where hope dwells, and pursue the creative ideal to be found in those who "hunger and thirst." *Blessed are the peacemakers, for they shall be called the children of God.*

Make us authentic. We will accept ourselves totally, unafraid of what we will find, even if it means to suffer abuse, ridicule or rejection. Only then can we change what can be changed. *Blessed are those who suffer persecution for the sake of righteousness, for theirs is the kingdom of heaven.*

The Church should be home for people. Calling the Church an institutions buoys images of aloofness and coldness. Father Pops made the Church home for many. He was an ordinary man, and he was empty enough and sufficiently poor to fill up on the Gospel challenge of Jesus' unconditional acceptance of self and others.

Father Pops didn't have to look for God. God found him, used him, and now, decades after his death, the fresh air he brought to the brokenhearted still soothes—at least this soul who is glad to have worked as a high school student in a rectory where ACCEPTANCE was written in capital letters, and in the ever-fresh face of fear-free Father Pops.

Decades after his demise and his class' continuance by others, my hope and dream is realized in the pearls for each day woven from Fr. Popielarz's eight binders of notes edited into a book that follows.

DAY 1

<u>Daily Act of Surrender</u>

I give unto Thee, O Lord, all that I am and have, committing heart, mind and soul to thy infinite power and grace. Free me from the prison of myself; the illusion of independence; and, the chains of sin. Make me an instrument of thy will and a humble apostle of Thy love. Now and forever. Amen.

DAY 2

If there is no meaning, there is nothing.

To be myself means to have found meaning.

DAY 3

"A man is always a teller of tales, He lives surrounded by his stories and the stories of others. He sees everything that happens to him through them, and tries to live his life as if he were recounting it"

Satre

DAY 4

If you are afraid to die, it means you are also afraid to live.
Because your "living" is bad, you consider dying as "bad." You
are fearful about death because you are fearful about life.
We become "free" or fearless by contact on a personal level.
Here we shed all forms of fear.

DAY 5

Help me **like** what I should do, O God, because with fear
present, I will ball-up the whole thing.

DAY 6

I will be happy only if I love; miserable if I hate or fear.

DAY 7

If I stop looking for happiness, I will find it.

DAY 8

Honesty deflates our feelings to the right size and position.

DAY 9

Awareness of self is your true North Star to steer your craft of
living.

DAY 10

The Bible says: "God so loved us, that He gave His only begotten Son."

Therefore God loves us. Right?

Right.

DAY 11

Whatever I think about myself becomes the measure of what others will think of me.

DAY 12

We must transcend our disability; we must become bigger than we are at the moment.

DAY 13

There is nothing "bad" in our human nature. Everything is good and we need everything. Stop conquering, destroying, fighting or cutting out people, things, ideas, possibilities.

DAY 14

When we are talented, we are potentially most creative. We will become neurotic unless we channel this creativity into our personal behavior also.

DAY 15

We must first detach ourselves from a loved one, in order to become attached properly, in order to resolve fear.

DAY 16

Everyone has his "snag" to find. Once found, learn to cope with it and then grow!

DAY 17

We must choose to be or not to be ourselves.

DAY 18

We all have an inherent capacity for guilt.

Guilt stems from aggression, i.e., by trying to get it "made." To "make it" you must victimize someone. Even though everyone is in this game, and we mutually and silently condone, still we feel guilty. We become overwhelmed by our own aggression.

DAY 19

One thing I must do alone: make a decision to "be" or "become" what I want.

DAY 20

There is no cure for a personal disorder. Accept, and then integrate your fault into your total being and now you are ready to apply "creative effort."

DAY 21

Alcoholism, like every personal disorder, is **the story of fear**.

Fear isolates us and cripples the capacity to love.

a) Fear makes me do what I shouldn't do.
Example: If I'm afraid I'll get drunk, almost certainly I will get drunk.

b) Fear keeps me from doing what I should do.
Example: Kept me from speaking easily to people. If I am fearful to speak, I will not speak.

DAY 22

The Bible tell me that Christ only cried once during His public life. (God is not a sentimentalist; He is a realist). He cried when he reflected on the **ingratitude** of His Chosen Race. By the way, it is the shortest verse in the whole Bible: "Jesus wept".

By pointing to **ingratitude** and crying, did Jesus want to point to the negative inner mechanism, from which all evil flows, all evil is born?

If so, when it would follow that indirectly He pointed to the positive inner mechanism that can repair any and all forms of non-physical harm done to the total man?

DAY 23

To be grateful means to be "other-centered."

But the alcoholic is compulsively self-centered, that is why he is spiritually and emotionally sick.

How can he become "other-centered"? By acting out gratitude.

DAY 24

When I arrived at Guest House I was told that I was 100% self-centered.

To change I must want; the prescription was simple, but oh so difficult: "don't you dare to think, feel or do anything for yourself. This is an order; this is a command."

DAY 25

It didn't make sense. Me self-centered? I gave all I had to ???
I blindly carried out orders.

Many a time did I make a fool of myself. I kept running around
the house, doing things for others, who like myself were sick
and not always welcomed my services, thinking I was "conning
them," like they were conning everyone else themselves before.

But slowly, I began to change; from a zombie I slowly began to
look like a human being; and from that a priest, I hope.

DAY 26

An attitude of gratitude is a pure prayer.

DAY 27

If you can reach the stage where you can give and keep giving
without one iota of "self-regard", you're an emotionally
mature guy.

DAY 28

Let the dead carry the dead.

DAY 29

Nothing reveals the weak spots of human nature better than humor.

DAY 30

When we "count" on love, it usually does not happen..

DAY 31

"My personality is acting up."

"The reason I did that is because, blah, blah!"

This "blame-placing" on someone other than self, is defensive behavior.

Try the "I am" instead of "I have" done so and so ... I have a demon.... I am sad because I do not "have" a position, a car, a good meal, a good meal, a good past, a good education.

Whatever problem I have, I am "it" – I am responsible for it!

DAY 32

I can carry the present; only God is strong enough to carry the other two dimensions of time, the past and the future.

DAY 33

There is a pathological fear in us of being "discovered" that we have a disorder, an ailment, a problem.

DAY 34

We must strive to become "loose" and not controlled, tight, fixed.

DAY 35

I am what I am by virtue of what I have and strive to have. The solution is to become what I am alone.

"Having" has for defenses these:

1) neurotic support
2) controls
3) pride

And these three are three forms of fear.

DAY 36

Don't separate your negative emotions. It's all one bag of beans and it is to be treated as an entity → our personality defect.

DAY 37

The more concerned I get about self, the more avenues of fear open up.

Fear holds me back from exposing myself.

DAY 38

Crucial question in therapy: "Do I want to change?" Just a glimmer of a desire is enough to generate hope of recovery.

Projecting is shifting the blame on another.

Nobody wins a personal fight!

DAY 39

If your thinking is fuzzy, work on your feelings. When you feel good, you think good and do good.

DAY 40

Accept what you are, be yourself, and you will change; even though you don't get rid of your problem! We get at the heart of the matter i.e. fear i.e. evil and get (anxious → a guilt-collector) rid of it eventually by empathy i.e. contact, recognition and acquaintance.

> In what the change? I drew out fear from self.
> "Do the thing you fear!"
> Wm. James.

DAY 41

Cavalier is synonymous with illogical. So now do what you feared to do without alcohol.

DAY 42

To be devoted expresses love at depth for something.

DAY 43

We can find meaning only through contact with others.

DAY 44

The thrill of recognition: a sense of community of belonging. We will "recognize" only when in contact with others.

DAY 45

When listening to another:

To understand, means to recognize, means to review a similar experience "semi-experience."

DAY 46

Once you exhaust the potential of "having," you will then ask "What's this all about?"

Now you are ready to look for something personal: freedom, creativity and empathy.

DAY 47

The very techniques I used to eliminate defenses are their meat: will-power.

DAY 48

Replace "fear" by "respect."

Fear – lack of drive to contact.

Fear is generic to all neurotic feelings: withdrawal, resentment, guilt, control, despair, self-sufficiency, rejection, loneliness.

After we visit a place the first time, it no longer seems far away.

DAY 49

A new movement is apparent every where, including the Church: "accept everything!"

DAY 50

Spiritual and the personality regulators:

The spiritual in our lives gives substance and structure to our personality regulators; it stabilizes them.

Neglect or drop the spiritual, and soon the contents of our conscience and super-ego will begin to dwindle.

DAY 51

We "become" when we act fear - freely. We "uncome" when we react fearfully.

DAY 52

There is a real skill in the simple techniques of "being." "How is the family?" This can cost us more in self-denial than pursuing "having" in the beginning.

DAY 53

Gratitude:

I have learned that gratitude is the only real and effective remedy for resentments.

DAY 54

An alcoholic fights his alcoholism when he continues to drink. He becomes free, when he stops drinking and accepts his powerlessness over alcohol.

DAY 55

Sensitive, childish and grandiose: the three basic qualities of an alcoholic.

DAY 56

There must be a tremendous deposit of Faith within each of us. Faith is basic to meaning.

DAY 57

Children will imitate a parent even as far as resentments toward the other parent.

To change the child's attitude change your own.

DAY 58

To free self of resentment or self-pity:

    1) communicate with others
    2) cultivate a sense of humor

DAY 59

Jealousy arises from possessiveness. Its expression makes worse the very situation we want to correct.

DAY 60

I can't cope with my problems all by myself. The idea of self-sufficiency is erroneous. NOT GOOD!

DAY 61

"Holy God, I give back to You whatever I have or hold: everyone, everything, and every place, including my self. Whatever you deign to will in my behalf from now on, I will accept with eternal gratitude. I only ask You for Your continued grace and infinite Love."

DAY 62

What do we worship most?

Check for what or whom you spend most of your money, when you are free to do so.

DAY 63

If you want hell, choose the dishonest one to associate with.

DAY 64

I will ask God and man only for what I need, not what I want.

DAY 65

The only thought that can madden or frighten me is one about self.

DAY 66

I must earn love; as a child I got it for nothing.

DAY 67

My decision will always be right, if I distinguish between what is important and what is not important.

DAY 68

Everything that happens is God's will, either by permission or by desire.

DAY 69

I will not limit my giving to those I like.

DAY 70

The more grateful I am the better and happier I become.
The more ungrateful I am, the worse and sadder I become.

DAY 71

Sometimes, God will use me as an actor to dramatize a
message, bitter or sweet, that could not be understood any
other way by myself or perhaps others.

DAY 72

When I am bugged, I will ventilate or end up hyper-ventilating,
and that is not good.

DAY 73

Don't be a leaf in the wind; become a wind of your own.

DAY 74

The rewards of honesty:

It modifies or corrects old notions.

DAY 75

The rewards of honesty:

It makes room for fresh and objectively true insights.

DAY 76

The rewards of honesty:

It empties us of the excrement's of our own error, injustice, pride and evil.

DAY 77

The rewards of honesty:

When I am honest, then my thinking, willing and feeling towards God, people and things is realistic, true, genuine and simple.

DAY 78

The rewards of honesty:

When dishonest, then my reactions are unrealistic, confusing, false, fake, exaggerated, complex and phony.

DAY 79

The rewards of honesty:

Like in art, there are only three simple figures in life: the line,
the angle and the circle. Dishonesty makes it complex; makes it
truly a "subjective piece of hodge-podge art."

DAY 80

Love is beyond the law; love is an out-law; love, and then do
as you like.

DAY 81

Our life together is one of invitation!

There are no musts!

DAY 82

We can hurt ourselves by overdoing in any area, save one, i.e.
in the spiritual.

DAY 83

Only God can we love with all our hearts, minds and souls.
Other people, only as ourselves.

DAY 84

When you are enjoying something totally, then only can you see God.

DAY 85

Meekness means willingness to learn, to draw in, open-mindedness, open-heartedness!

DAY 86

He who seeks the right ways has "right-wiseness."

DAY 87

Almighty and eternal Father, we assemble here with bowed heads and hopeful hearts, are trying to discharge out debt of gratitude to You.

We wish to thank you for the AA program and for your graces that helped us use it as a therapy in our recovery from the disease of alcoholism.

May Your power deliver us, Your wisdom lead us and Your presence calm us.

And dear Lord, grant us the serenity to accept the things we cannot change, the courage to change the things we can, and the wisdom to know the difference. Amen

DAY 88

I feel a resentment when you are not "acting as I want."

Resentment is an insult to God. In "Moby Dick," Ashad shakes his fist at God.

When we help someone recognize what's wrong in a relationship we have succeeded.

DAY 89

These result from the dilemmas of the drive of fear in human desires:

    1) Anxiety
    2) Depression (disorders of the self: having: human desires. "I want that!" "What's my angle?")
    3) Withdrawal

DAY 90

It doesn't make it good to be aware of a defect and still indulge in it. But it makes it less sick and pathetic.

DAY 91

The brighter I am, the sicker I can be personally and the more distant the cure!

DAY 92

You can't solve a personal problem intellectually.

DAY 93

"Know yourself" – this is out moded. We can find ourselves only through contact with others.

DAY 94

If our defenses are up, we can't be in touch, even though we are in contact.

DAY 95

We are disordered in a certain area, when we lose freedom in that area.

DAY 96

To be young we must be free!

DAY 97

I can carry anybody's load except my own; only God can carry mine.

DAY 98

If I want to check what is wrong with me, all I have to do is study the faults of those I dislike.

DAY 99

Every sin is a form of pampering and pampering is for infants.

DAY 100

When I am unhappy, I do something for another and not myself.

DAY 101

I will be happy if I stop crying about everything except one thing: my sins.

DAY 102

It is a child's right to receive; the nature of a grown-up demands that he be a giver.

DAY 103

I have two enemies: self-centeredness and stubbornness and they are what can make me stupid.

DAY 104

The only thing I can give God is my willingness to receive: i.e. His Will and His Grace.

DAY 105

Jean Paul Sarte: "Beware of generous people" – they will take you for all you got. Beware of the reasons for the giving.

DAY 106

Resort to your sense of humor when you become aware that you are being used.

DAY 107

Let people be nice to you. By accepting you give them opportunity to be kind.

DAY 108

We are prone to equate all in terms of quantity.

DAY 109

The only things that make up my "I am" are the areas where I am defective.

DAY 110

We must join a group "bigger" than ourselves.

DAY 111

Friendship is based on defect.

DAY 112

It's not what one knows, but what one does.

DAY 113

It's not in how one thinks, but what one feels.

DAY 114

It's not the height of one's body, but the depth of one's soul.

DAY 115

It's not how high will one reach to receive, but how low one will stoop to give.

DAY 116

One is quick to compromise a policy, but never a principle.

DAY 117

One is thankful for what one has, and grateful for what one can give.

DAY 118

One strives not for cleverness, but for wisdom.

DAY 119

One would rather be right, than be popular.

DAY 120

One will never trade one's self-respect for one's respect.

DAY 121

One prefers to make 10 costly mistakes in judgment, than one mistake in charity.

DAY 122

We must become single-minded, if we are to arrest our past.

DAY 123

Single-mindedness is tolerance without fear and hate.

DAY 124

If the angels blush with shame it is when they behold an ungrateful person. They cover their faces with their wings and weep because the most sacred thing we can give to another, our love, he has desecrated.

DAY 125

A priest wrote this letter to one who had "conned" him:

Thank you for giving me the last lecture in your course on Ingratitude. It was the most costly course I had ever taken in my life. It cost me everything I had: money, job, position, reputation and almost my life. It was worth it, because it acquainted me with the most hideous and diabolical misuse of human love. You had to give me almost a lethal dose of it to show me its real ugliness. Upon reflection, I can now see how ungrateful I was to so many people I will use the few remaining years left to make up the past, by never taking for granted, let alone misusing the most sacred thing another can offer me: his love. On bended knees from now on will I gratefully accept the smallest gesture of love, as though I was receiving the Sacrament itself – the sacrament instituted by Christ to groom us properly to be able to love and to be able to be loved.

DAY 126

Neglect or drop the spiritual, and soon the contents of one's conscience and super-ego will begin to dwindle.

DAY 127

To help another, one uses not the toughness of one's mind, but the gentleness of one's heart.

DAY 128

One is an acolyte in the Cathedral of the Spirit, lighting the taper of illumination from the fire of one's own redemption.

DAY 129

One knows that if one's lamp of charity burns dim, the light of hope for another may go out forever.

DAY 130

Daily one lights a candle of hope from the flame of compassion which must burn steadily in the sanctuary of every true heart.

DAY 131

Because each had kept one's rendezvous with fate, now together one can hold high date with destiny.

DAY 132

Thank you for letting me give.

DAY 133

You can't be free or real or meaningful, alone.

DAY 134

Psychological youth, freedom and meaning are the ultimate.

DAY 135

Infants and old folks are imprisoned, helpless, dependent and lonely.

DAY 136

How to realize goal of our creation?

We were created in order to become united with God. But before this is possible we must become "another Christ".

To effect this we must follow the same pattern that His Son did in order to become Man.

Like He, we need the Holy Spirit and the Blessed Virgin.

We need to be overshadowed by the spirit and then grow in the bosom of Mary.

DAY 137

Two groups here: contented and discontented.

If you are contented, is your contentment built on a foundation that "moth cannot eat, rust cannot corrode, and thieves cannot steal?"

DAY 138

If your contentment is not secure, then you are no better off than those here present who are discontented. It is only a matter of time and you too will be discontented.

DAY 139

Alcoholism is a disease that makes me powerless over alcohol.

DAY 140

Like no other disease known, it affects my total being.

DAY 141

Recovery demands treatment of the total man: physical, emotional, and spiritual.

DAY 142

Treat only one phase and I will not recover.

DAY 143

Medicine alone, psychology alone, religion alone, will not make me well.

DAY 144

Because AA advocates using all three disciplines, that is why it is successful.

DAY 145

AA tells me to use medicine as a therapy
psychology as a therapy
religion as a therapy. -

DAY 146

If you feel resentful, come out with it; don't harbor it. This helps dynamics of recognition.

DAY 147

Recognize your feelings and say-so! Hugging it only makes it worse.

DAY 148

Human behavior is based on feelings and not logic.

DAY 149

What you feel is more important than what you know.

DAY 150

"Like God, in the story of the Prodigal Son, I will love you so much, that I will permit you to go to the very brink of Hell; if you should decide to return, know that I'll be waiting for you with outstretched arms".

DAY 151

We must learn to be:

    1) free
    2) resourceful (Ideals of being: I want to be myself)
    3) sharing

DAY 152

Imitation: I become serene by imitating serene people; sober by imitating sober people.

DAY 153

We can learn to be acquainted with one another in a group situation.

DAY 154

"Free-imitation" – we do not escape, but freely choose what we like about the other. There is no "imposed" imitation!

DAY 155

I am not imitating any thing at all, if I don't have a lot of respect for you. Without respect, I will lack the want to imitate.

DAY 156

We gain self-respect by respecting others.

DAY 157

I recognize in you what I have or have a potential for; otherwise, I could not recognize.

DAY 158

One can sense good-will in others even if he never shows any toward others, because the potential to be good-will is in all of us!

DAY 159

First we imitate many and eventually develop our own style.

DAY 160

Don't limit "imitating" to one same age stage. Do it all your life.

DAY 161

"Don't read any more; go to people!" (advice given to Dr. David Stewart by his teacher)

DAY 162

"I'm a people watcher," meaning: a good psychologist.

DAY 163

The same principles regarding free imitation can be applied to things, like art, music, writing.

DAY 164

Most addicts will deny their guilt; after six months all admitted it. A point came when they admitted that what they did was rotten from both the standpoint of God and society; they did this once they came to the conclusion that theirs is a disease; that there was hope for salvation; hope for a change. Then they can recover.

DAY 165

Conscious guilt is the business of religion.

DAY 166

Unconscious guilt is the business of psychiatry and psychology.

DAY 167

The more "personable" I am, then the more genuinely selfish I am.

DAY 168

When I draw myself alone, it becomes awfully boring.

DAY 169

Self-love and respect are necessary for abundant living!

DAY 170

Support – control – pride = 3 losses!

These losses are conditions for freedom, creativity and empathy!

DAY 171

Guilt can bring on such horrifying symptoms in a human being, that in the middle ages, these symptoms became synonymous with being in the possession of the devil.

DAY 172

Thanks to the development of medicine, sinfulness is less and less attributed to one form of illness or another. This does not mean that we will remove the moral aspect of a disease even if we label it a disease.

DAY 173

Why so hard to admit that one is an alcoholic?

It would mean to identify:

1. intellectually with a fool
2. emotionally with a child
3. morally with a degenerate
4. spiritually with an atheist

DAY 174

I don't say that anyone reaches all these extremes. But as humans we either think in universals or particulars. A drunk. This drunk.

DAY 175

When we are faced with doing something about our drinking, the universal notion of a drunk comes to mind: the drunk-supreme.

DAY 176

The greatest sin is ingratitude:

The second greatest is attaching an ulterior motive to our giving.

DAY 177

"Beware of the Greeks bearing gifts".

DAY 178

God is giving, nature is giving, animals are giving.

DAY 179

Only man, when driven by a perverse compulsory self-centeredness is "taking".

DAY 180

Motivation and gratitude:

The will is free, but it will not move by itself. It is potentially free.

DAY 181

The best mover is gratitude because it comes from a memory that tugs at the heart-strings.

DAY 182

We became sick or neurotic because whatever we did was for self or for a self-regarding motive.

DAY 183

To get well we must "do" for "other" regarding reasons, even when we must do something for self. I will shave, the family will like my being considerate.

DAY 184

Free self of all angles. Give without any expectation of return. Never anticipate or care for reciprocation, let alone demand it.

DAY 185

It is the business of the Church to make people happy, for true happiness is true holiness.

DAY 186

It is wrong to say that one must be unhappy here, if he expects to be happy in eternity. Accordingly, Christ had to teach us how to be happy here and now, and this He did by giving us the Eight Beatitudes.

DAY 187

"Get between your kid and drugs anyway you can. If you want to save their life".

Carol O'Connor, actor

DAY 188

When discussing the use of alcohol, ministers often exhibit greater prejudice and hostility than in discussing race or religion. For this reason, it is imperative that the disease concept of alcoholism be understood.

DAY 189

Effective counseling on alcoholism begins with an understanding of the illness, and acceptance of the alcoholic as a sick person.

DAY 190

Alcoholics have an abounding guilt, real and neurotic. This is frequently projected toward the minister who, in their mind, is God's "executive officer," or at least his "first sergeant." No matter how much skill the minister may develop, and despite evidence of his deep concern for alcoholics, this feeling will usually remain. Many alcoholics would rather have the sheriff come for arrest rather than the minister for a visit. The minister must accept the fact that, initially, he may be the last person who should attempt counseling a particular alcoholic and be willing to let others render this service.

DAY 191

By his entire attitude and his preaching, the minister can help establish a climate which is conducive to shame and concealment of the illness, or, on the other hand, can help create understanding and initiate an open attack upon **the disease** rather than upon the alcoholic.

DAY 192

The greater your unselfishness, the greater become all of your horizons: time, people, places and things.

DAY 193

Much better to have AA get you. Everything then becomes more meaningful: people, places and things.

DAY 194

Other anxiety reducers: smoking, obesity, work, pills. All will have fine funeral except alcoholic. Why? Because his is a behavior disease.

DAY 195

Alcoholic is allergic to sin. Horrible guilt threshold.

DAY 196

Needs to drink are created only by evil. Craving to drink will disappear when good conquers.

DAY 197

An alcoholic contaminates everybody and everything he touches. It's not true of any other disease.

DAY 198

People below 40 years old accept that alcoholism is a disease.

DAY 199

People above 40, only the minority does; they are the stinkers who need educating.

DAY 200

We don't take the disease of alcoholism seriously enough; it is the number 1 disease of humankind all over the world.

DAY 201

Half of AA membership does not believe that it is a disease.

DAY 202

Bishops of America: intellectual consent, but not emotional. "Moral-weakness" aspect is still looming large in their minds.

DAY 203

Other diseases are cured by others; not so with addiction; it can be stopped only by the individual himself; that is why it is so painful; it demands a total change of one's personality.

DAY 204

Outsiders can see the immediate signs of other illnesses, but not of alcoholism; the alcoholic must show secondary symptoms, before they are noticed; behavior pattern.

DAY 205

What disease aspect did for me.

Only after I realized that alcoholism is a disease is it possible to stop hating self, because then one sees that he was not 100% responsible for the insane things he felt, thought and did. Once his disease is arrested, I feel that the inner resources implanted during my good years, my present new insights and especially with the aid of God's grace I dare to hope that the future can be promising.

DAY 206

People want to be happy, but instead of using Christ's means, they follow the world's advice, or their own inclinations.

DAY 207

Christ's way to happiness is based on unselfishness, while the world's, on selfishness.

DAY 208

Consider created things as means and not as ends.

DAY 209

Man was created to love, obey, and serve God, and by so doing, to save his own soul. But in order to do this, he must use created things. Therefore, we may6 use all good created things, providing we do not make them ends in themselves.

DAY 210

Why did Christ give us the eight Beatitudes?

1. As God, Christ knew that man due to Original Sin finds it difficult to be happy, and that it was up to Him, as the Messiah to give us the way.

2. As man, Christ practiced the Beatitudes, and found them to be effective, since He had inner contentment and never soured at life.

DAY 211

"Blessed are the poor in spirit, for theirs is the Kingdom of Heaven".

This Beatitude gives us the following principle:

Anyone who for the sake of God develops the habit of detachment from persons, places and things – he will be happy.

DAY 212

To be poor in Spirit does not mean:

1. That one must necessarily be without comforts and money.
2. That one cannot have a good position or a good time.
3. That one cannot have friends or loved ones.

DAY 213

If we want to satisfy the Commandment of Love, our love must be unselfish.

DAY 214

If our love is selfish, we will unconsciously be kind and considerate only to a few, i.e. only to those we like. Why? Because doing good to one we like gives us self-satisfaction.

DAY 215

Charity demands that every Catholic tender minimum forms of courtesy to all people, irrespective how we may feel about them.

DAY 216

To love or to hope in man?

It is one thing to love man, and still another to place one's hope in him; the difference so great that the first is commanded while the second is forbidden. (St. Augustine)

DAY 217

Why should we not become too attached?

Because life being what it is, we might loose or might be forced to leave the place, thing or person to whom we have become unduly attached, and as a result will become miserable and unhappy.

DAY 218

Accentuate the positive, and eliminate the negative.

Our religion wants us to be positive and not negative characters. This is in agreement with natural law, because our whole being craves doing things. Thus, in working out your salvation, spend your days doing good, rather than remaining inactive, thus trying to avoid evil.

DAY 219

Ideal Poverty

The most perfect kind of poverty is not the one that strips you of things, but the one that strips you of all attachments. St. Augustine puts it this way, "Real poverty is in the soul, and not in the person".

DAY 220

It is difficult for the very poor to become poor in spirit.

To develop the spirit of poverty, we need the minimum of comfort and security. Dire poverty is a kind of hell, it exposes too the sin, lowers our spirits, and develops over-anxiety.

DAY 221

You will find happiness by not looking for it.

Naturally speaking, the only way we can look for happiness is by following our own impulses or the world's advice, and these contrary to our expectations never make us really happy. Stop following these, and in their place fulfill your obligations, and you will slowly, but surely, find happiness.

DAY 222

God created all things good.

Avoid the heretical notion that most things are bad in themselves. Therefore, things such as movies, comforts, positions, etc., but over-anxiety for these things is bad.

DAY 223

We live in an age that fosters over anxiety for things.

From the point of view of a salesman, consumptionism is the science of compelling people to want, to buy and to use more and more things. This philosophy is painlessly but effectively inculcating in us by way of magazine, billboards and radio commercials and it is all too apparent that we all yield.

DAY 224

Human Nature is resourceful.

Let us not forget that human nature has tremendous possibilities for making one happy. The tragedy is that people seldom develop these possibilities, and as a result are unhappy, thinking that if their physical appearance or if their mental capacities and position were different, they would be happy.

The moment we reach the stage, when things, people, and places cease to disturb us, they lose their power to cause suffering, and as a result, we can be happy without them.

DAY 225

"Blessed are the meek; for they shall possess the land."

The first Beatitude asks us to free ourselves from the domination of things outside of ourselves, while the second Beatitude asks us to free ourselves from the domination of "self".

DAY 226

What is humility?

Humility is truth that is seeing oneself in correct relation to God, people and things.

DAY 227

What is meekness?

Humility is an attitude of the mind, while meekness is the manifestation of the attitude. Meekness is self control; it is the restraining from the selfish use of the passions.

DAY 228

Emotional immaturity harms physical and spiritual health.

DAY 229

From fear and anger change to love motives.

DAY 230

From servitude to service.

DAY 231

From must and ought to want.

DAY 232

Change the changeable and accept the unchangeable.

DAY 233

Physical health is involuntary.

DAY 234

Emotional and spiritual health is at our command.

DAY 235

Therefore: health, maturity and virtue are the ingredients of the formula for happiness.

DAY 236

Creative skill and an addiction – one has freedom, choice, discipline, the other has none of these.

DAY 237

"I don't want to get rid of anything, because I need everything I have": good attitude.

DAY 238

To re-direct my "problem" traits into other channels, is the idea.

DAY 239

A lawyer got his client a suspended sentence – they hanged him!

DAY 240

You make a senseless action sensible by saying: "I am now going to make myself miserable!" Do it deliberately.

DAY 241

"Greater love than this no man hath, that a man lay down his life for a friend. I have not called you servants, but I have called you friends." Therefore, Christ, God as I understand Him, loves us.

DAY 242

The religion to which I have dedicated my life, teaches that the greatest sin one of its adherents can commit is to question God's love.

DAY 243

All right, since God loves us with an infinite love and since millions of people suffer from character disorders – not only alcoholics – when He created man He had to put into him an inner mechanism, which if put into action will repair any damage in personality which man in a stupid spree, lasting one, five, ten or fifty years, brought about.

DAY 244

Does gratitude trigger off the growth of all virtues in man?

Does ingratitude trigger off the growth of all vices in man?

What is gratitude?

An acknowledgment and warm feeling of appreciation for something received. Sacrifice of self, effort, time or possessions.

DAY 245

Typical behavior of alcoholic:

The alcoholic gets from A and gives to as many C's as his deposit of "goodies" permits. He never gives back to A, unless to save face.

DAY 246

As the alcoholic keeps giving to all the B's, A keeps giving keeps caring, keeps following and gets infuriated by the minute.

DAY 247

Soon what was given to the alcoholic in charity he begins to expect in justice. What's this? Where's my money? My clothes? My food? My drink? My position? My reputation? (I was disgusting).

DAY 248

Eventually A stops and holds us giving. Alcoholic is remorseful and begs forgiveness. A forgives and alcoholic begins again. All is fine for a while. But wait. Now he really has a chance to be ungrateful again, but good. He has a real "launching pad, the cat." And again he drinks, because A did or said or thought or felt something. It was that that triggered off his drinking. You bet. He had the arms with which to start a new rebellion.

DAY 249

Again an empasse. Alcoholic is miserable and so is A.

DAY 250

Alcoholic tells his buddies: "if A would only change; would only get squared away. So A hopefully gives him another chance. The same story: Alcoholic drinks again. Both forgot that Alcoholic must change and not A.

DAY 251

Yes, the alcoholic must begin with those who loved and kept giving to him. He kept running away from those who loved him and those who kept giving to him.

DAY 252

On the other hand, he was giving to those who were running away from him. Talk about a rat-race.

He must stop. Make an about face and begin giving to those who have been giving to him.

DAY 253

We become like the one to whom we give.

We were becoming more and more frustrated, because we kept giving to those who kept running away from us.

DAY 254

The same for our loved ones. The more they gave, the faster we ran and more frustrated they became.

DAY 255

Justice-gratitude is giving to those who have given to us.

Charity-gratitude is giving to those who have not given to us.

DAY 256

If we continue to give only to the "have given nots", ignoring our "have givens", we will disturb our conscience, disturb our serenity. Besides, how else are we going to make amends to those we hurt by frustration, confusion, doubt and neglect?

DAY 257

Last word: the less "self-regarding" is our gratitude, the more effective therapy it is. The more "self-regarding", the less effective.

DAY 258

Austin Ripley calls gratitude the memory of the heart; the inspiration to charity; the golden tray on which we hand to man the things we received from God.

DAY 259

Following the prompting of that memory, we will begin to
repay slowly but surely God and man for having given to us.

DAY 260

We will rid ourselves of all faults and automatic virtues, the
definition of which we do not know or have to know, will
begin to sprout within you.

DAY 261

From a "self-regarding" bad guy you will become an "other-
centered" good guy.

Therefore if you want humility, unselfishness, patience, etc.,
give.

DAY 262

It's easy for me to now see that one of the horrible ravages
which alcohol did to my person is that it almost destroyed my
honesty.

DAY 263

What is honesty? Webster gives many definitions, synonyms:

One who will not lie, cheat or steal
Being what it seems
Genuine
Pure

DAY 264

Faithful adherence to the ethical principles that are expected of one in his social class, profession or position.

DAY 265

We must discover in our lives "some sense of meaning." Then develop technique through discipline.

Meaning: "Is life worth living?" "What's this all about?"

DAY 266

I will pray and strive for what I need, not what I want.

DAY 267

I found myself, only because God permitted me to lose myself.

DAY 268

The only thought that can anger or frighten me is one about myself.

DAY 269

I must earn love; as a child I got it for nothing.

DAY 270

As a child I accepted qualified authority; now I must accept authority for the sake of authority.

DAY 271

My decision will be right, if I distinguish between what is important and what is unimportant.

DAY 272

Everything happens of God's will, either by permission or intent.

DAY 273

Carry your defect into your new way of life. There is such a thing as healthy anxiety, guilt, loneliness and depression.

DAY 274

"A man's religion is what he does with his solitude."
                                              Whitely

DAY 275

Tillich: There is an existential need for anxiety, depression and loneliness!

DAY 276

Ambition: Object of drive is me and not the object of my pursuit.

DAY 277

I'm in love with what I love and I'm not interested in the image.

DAY 278

Duty is doing what I ought; and love is doing what I must, I want!

DAY 279

We do not have all the answers in our human setting. We must base certain acceptances on Faith.

DAY 280

Deeply disordered persons basically, have lost Faith. They can't muster enthusiasm, meaning or feeling, because the human setting alone cannot give them these.

DAY 281

We want to fulfill self and we wind up anxious, depressed and withdrawn. A paradox.

DAY 282

We become personal when there is a contact between my "self" and your "self."

DAY 283

We have been so busy pursuing "having" that we have no idea of the thrill of pursuing "being."

DAY 284

The art of "small-talk" is worth striving for.

DAY 285

"Having" has to do with "preserving."

DAY 286

"Being" has to do with "growing."

DAY 287

Show me a non-neurotic and I will show you a grateful and humble person.

DAY 288

My psychiatric experience with the gadgets which make our minds work reinforce this gratitude. That is why I am grateful for these mental mechanisms and look upon them as gifts from God. These permit me to forget, to sublimate, to rationalize, to day-dream, to project and introject.

DAY 289

My present faith has defined reality to mean more than my house or office or community. My faith has extended the definition of reality to include the supernatural world – for which I am now trying to prepare myself by remembering that Power that I once was as greater than I – and lost – and then found again.

DAY 290

Contact means communication at depth, without engaging.

DAY 291

The quality of our contacts will differ in degree.

DAY 292

Be intimate but with respect.

DAY 293

By nature, people are either givers or takers, until they get the insight to become both.

DAY 294

A boner is a howler, a misprint, a right word in the wrong place (or vice versa), a slight error in association that turns a simple fact into a side-splitting absurdity.

DAY 295

It is better for a minister who finds that alcoholics anger him or disgust him to accept this and not counsel them but, rather, know how and to whom to refer them.

DAY 296

The same is true for ministers who begin to enjoy the alcoholic's dependency needs, or feel very uncomfortable because he is unable to meet these needs.

DAY 297

Continued support of an alcoholic should never be the goal of pastoral counseling.

DAY 298

Long-term supportive therapy is not the ideal.

DAY 299

It is more important to teach a man how to get up than to pick him up, to encourage him to walk than to carry him along.

DAY 300

Changing the attitude of the family often can help the alcoholic more than by directly counseling him.

DAY 301

Often wives may cover up and refuse to acknowledge the husband's alcoholism, because of a sense of shame and disgrace.

DAY 302

Facing the wife of an alcoholic has a dual task. Securing an open admission of the existence of alcoholism the wife's involvement may be so intense that she may present a more acute pastoral problem than her husband.

DAY 303

The wife may even attempt to use the minister as a tool to fulfill her more neurotic needs.

DAY 304

The wife cannot become her husband's therapist.

DAY 305

If she can begin to understand her own emotional involvement and begin to unravel her own tangled emotions, then, and only then, will she be in a position to deal adequately with the husband's drinking problem.

DAY 306

Self-improvement, therefore, is by far the best method she can employ in helping her husband initially.

DAY 307

One of the most difficult tasks for the minister is to refrain from trying to prevent what he feels may be wrong.

DAY 308

If the minister intervenes or tries to thwart the normal process of events, he may well prevent the very crisis out of which a vital decision may be made and which could even lead to a permanent solution of the problem.

DAY 309

The minister's role is not to make decisions, but rather to interpret what is happening.

DAY 310

Neither advise separation or attempt to prevent it.

DAY 311

If separation occurs do not attempt to promote quick, easy reconciliation.

DAY 312

By refusing to remain under these conditions, she may very well bring the drinking to an end, then she is completely justified in considering separation as a means of helping her husband to face reality, and start recovery.

DAY 313

If a wife gives her husband a choice of seeking help for alcoholism or of accepting his continual drinking as a breach of marriage, she is being realistic, not unfair.

DAY 314

It is possible for a wife to leave her husband in love rather than waiting for her love to be destroyed.

DAY 315

If the wife leaves in fear she will return to anxiety. If she leaves in anger she will return in embarrassment and resentment. If, however, she leaves in love she may return at any point when conditions have sufficiently changed to make a genuine reconciliation possible.

DAY 316

If you try to take the bottle away from the alcoholic or the alcoholic away from the bottle, you are wasting your time and effort.

DAY 317

You are unique. You have all the "givens" to be supremely happy.

DAY 318

The sufferer is the unnecessary martyr. This person, regardless of age, education, social or economic level thrives on "bleeding emotionally" in order to secure gratification.

DAY 319

Suicide is an extreme form of hostility for, by this single act, one kills every existing person.

DAY 320

In a symbolic sense she is asking for crucifixion and by the shedding of her blood will, thereby, save her husband from his sin of drinking.

DAY 321

The "sufferer" should not get praise, sympathy or comfort.

DAY 322

In kindness and firmness, she must be shown that she is trying to enter God's area of action.

DAY 323

The punisher or sadist plays the opposite role from the sufferer. Perhaps this trait is less destructive than masochism in that it can be seen more easily, and thus the husband can fight back. Sadists need some person to punish, and for many a sadistic spouse of an alcoholic fulfills this need perfectly. One wife, after four years of adequate therapy stated, "I realize now that every time my husband got sober, I tripped him up in order to provoke his drinking again. Each time he drank I could prove to the whole world, through him, what stinkers all men were." A wife may punish her husband repeatedly and in innumerable ways. It has been said that some of the meanest women in the world are married to alcoholics.

DAY 324

The controller may be more difficult to recognize. The wife, to remove herself from a state of utter confusion, assumes the role of the head of the house and manager of the family situation. Control may be an expedient which the wife feels is an absolute necessity to save the family – and this is often true. But it can also be (or become) a desperate need of her own, apart from any realistic connection with the alcoholism situation. The dependency needs of the alcoholic play right into the hands of a controlling wife, and rarely can these dependency needs be broken unless the source of the dependency is willing to make a complete change and relinquish control.

DAY 325

The wavering wife must be given to understand that her ambivalence and impulsive actions are as irrational and destructive as her husband's compulsive drinking. If necessary use direct and specific instructions against any known and destructive action patterns. Try to set up every counseling session as a learning process against impulsive action and always give support to well-planned decisions.

DAY 326

St. Paul: "The letter kills, the spirit frees."

DAY 327

Laws and prohibitions worsened rather than improved my defects. Guide-lines are the answer.

DAY 328

People with high spirited gumption will do when told not to and vice-versa.

DAY 329

We must become devoted to something; we must fall in love with something. Only then will we lose our need and want to drink, not to steal, etc.

DAY 330

The period of regret, mourning, and distress, for some, is short, for others long.

DAY 331

Don't let mourning become chronic and lingering.

DAY 332

Life is for the living. After a needed period of mourning, resume living.

DAY 333

When mourning becomes chronic, it no longer is a sign of love, but of self-pity.

DAY 334

To protract a mourning is to continue a dependence.

DAY 335

The "departed" one would want us to stop crying and "get with it" with living, "you have a job to do."

DAY 336

There is value in suffering if we see it as a means to insight.

DAY 337

Suffering in itself is useless.

DAY 338

Law, by its very nature produces an atmosphere of fear. Principle or guide-line, on the other hand, produces an atmosphere of love. The first makes us slaves; the second friends.

DAY 339

You were not only born an individual, but you keep "birthing" your individuality.

DAY 340

Again and again, Pops would say to me: Whatever our situation, we only have one problem that we all face - FEAR! Showing up for the Class in Acceptance became a staple in my life, and at first, I was confused by it and yet drawn to it all at the same time. Gradually, as I stayed the course, my life began to shift while the power of my demons receded.
Fr. Frederick J. Klettner

DAY 341

I can't give more to you, than you can to me. All encounters are reciprocal in effects.

Three degrees of likeness:

      1) like all other → in sickness
      2) like some others → in convalescence
      3) unlike others → in health

Watch and learn who have a good thing going in spite of their defects.

DAY 342

Develop as many skills as possible. Become versatile; potential is unlimited.

DAY 343

We find technique through disposition toward a situation to be coped with it.

DAY 344

We find discipline through commitment. Before we drop an addiction, we must fall in love with something better. A "wholesale-commitment." In the interim you can "woo" a situation just as you can a girl.

DAY 345

You remain yourself if you imitate freely.

DAY 346

From the beginning an imposed imitation is necessary, since we must begin with a starting point that is not ours.

DAY 347

Self-sufficiency is the opposite of discipline.

DAY 348

Discipline is always inter-personal.

DAY 349

"To love" is an experience to strive for.

DAY 350

If I resent you I can't get to know you or self; fear distorts perception.

DAY 351

I must be well-disposed toward you, for my own sake.

DAY 352

All intimacy must be balanced by respect.

DAY 353

I must live lovingly every difficulty.

DAY 354

When I fight my disorder, I give it strength.

DAY 355

Meaning is always a principle of action.

DAY 356

To be happy does not mean "to be pleased."

DAY 357

To be free is an important as "being pleased" – the first always present in happiness, the second is most contingent.

DAY 358

What technique is so and so using? Observe and imitate and eventually bring in creativity.

DAY 359

A group of us can do something so much better than one or two of us.

DAY 360

There is no place for comparisons.

DAY 361

Fellowship based on defects, then there is no fear; based on assets, then it's "edgy."

DAY 362

Be "man enough"; be responsible for your choice to drink orange juice when everyone else is drinking whiskey and you can't.

DAY 363

Once you can get beneath the surface and understand the actual nature of his life, you will discover that the alcoholic has been sinned against more than he has sinned.

DAY 364

Ministers probably have more opportunity than any other professional person for helping the alcoholic, and may do this, by counseling with the family, employer and others, without even once talking to the alcoholic in person.

DAY 365

It is easy and enjoyable to deal, associate, work or play with an honest person.

> "Perhaps the long delayed publication of Fr. Popielarz's wisdom is providential. Maybe the Catholic world wasn't ready for him then. Now, however, it is quite ready to cherish his wisdom and blend it into our life."
>
> Fr. Andrew M. Greeley

To judge and to explain is to be afraid.

A personal disorder is best understood or treated by first accepting it and further exploring its meaning in the experience of contact. Most of us initiate habits or disorders, not as a result of any clear-cut cause, motive or stimulus, but in search of personal meaning. Contact has to be made in order to understand the problem and to cope with it. Such contact always requires contact both with my problem and with another person, and always the meaning of my problem is to be found in me, not outside or independent of me.

The way to freedom, to personal meaning, is found by becoming responsible for myself. Becoming responsible begins in accepting myself "evil" and all, defects along with merits. If I do not accept my defect, I will be stuck with the defenses which make it impossible for me to be responsible for myself. I make a decisive start in freedom when I face the truth that by myself I am powerless. When I communicate to you the stark truth that I am nothing by myself there is born the hope that I can be free, without limits, in contact with a vitalizing agent in touch with my former isolated impotent self. In accepting my disorder, I undergo a change of heart. The thing, person, disorder, or whatever it is I accept, does not change, but I do. In this change I grow free. Liberated from total involvement on the plane of Having, I feel and act differently on the plane of Being.

Freedom from my disorder comes from feeling differently about the problem, not from knowing better. I feel value where once I sensed only fear. I give myself over to an attitude other than the fearful one in which I fought, struggled, escaped or played a role in the power game. This new attitude is good will. The meaning of the disorder deepens and reveals more to me than it did formerly for it is now grounded in good will, the source of my freedom.

Genuine contact with my problem gives me its meaning, its principle of action. There are two aspects of its principle of action: a) The reason the problem developed; b) The goal it moves toward, no matter what. The reason of my disorder, or the purpose for which I did what I did, was to be free and easy, relaxed from fear, relaxed, at one with others, at peace with myself, comfortable - in a word, to be happy. Yet, this reason, which was originally sound, became distorted by the defensive supports as my disorder moved towards its goal - unhappiness. Now my disorder means "search for happiness in the absence of freedom."

DYNAMICS OF ACCEPTANCE AS CONTAINED IN CHRIST'S BEATITUDES (Mt. 5: 2-12)

LOSS OF SUPPORT - CONTACT - FREEDOM

1. Blessed are the poor in spirit, for theirs is the kingdom of heaven. Personable.
2. Blessed are they who mourn, for they shall be comforted. Active.

LOSS OF CONTROL - RECOGNITION - CREATIVE EFFORT

3. Blessed are the meek, for they shall possess the earth. Trainable.
4. Blessed are they that hunger and thirst for justice, for they shall be satisfied. Practical.
5. Blessed are the merciful, for they shall obtain mercy. Compassionate.

LOSS OF BEING "LOVED" - ACQUAINTANCE - LOVE

6. Blessed are the pure of heart, for they shall see God. Single-minded.
7. Blessed are the peacemakers, for they shall be called children of God. Imaginative.

COURAGE TO BE YOURSELF

8. Blessed are they who suffer persecution for the sake of righteousness, for theirs is the kingdom of heaven. Authentic.

SEVEN NECESSARY PRINCIPLES FOR GROWTH IN PRIESTHOOD

1. As a human being, I am powerless alone, therefore, I must accept the loss of old supports.
2. As a human being, I control myself and others in vain, therefore I must accept the loss of control.
3. As a human being, I am self-sufficient and lonely, therefore I must accept the loss of love.
4. As a person, I contact others who help me to be free, in detachment and touch.
5. As a person I recognize others who inspire me to be creative, through insight and participation.
6. As a person I become acquainted with others, models who show me the interplay of respect and intimacy.
7. As a person, I put myself in your place, in order to develop my own style in favorite interests, to learn from you how to be myself . . .I learn also to see myself as "the other" sees me.

THE DILEMNA OF SELF-INTOXICATION

When fear feeds fear (conflict=withdrawal=isolation= confusion) in a circular poisonous process, it can be called self-intoxication. To be caught in this state is to experience frustrating confusion in which I am unable to understand my feelings and unable to distinguish between defenses and ideals. Search for causes, for cures, and the painful experience of will power only serves to worsen this "dry-dunk."

To get out of this mess, to find myself, to rediscover meaning, I have to make a personal decision. I have to decide "to be free". Decision is the future in the present, the ideal in action. It is myself, all of me, in an expression of what I am. Such a decision does not put me at war with myself. The decisive center of my person must determine whether I am to thrive in freedom, or sink into personal disorder.

The decision "to be free" must be followed by a decision to "resist not evil". Such a decision must be renewed daily because "it does not keep". "To resist not evil" means to "stop fighting," "discipline yourself" and "to accept". "Evil" here is a word of personal meaning. Anything I regard as injurious, unpleasant, painful to my living as I want to live is evil. We defend ourselves against what we suspect will harm us. This suspicion arises from fear ("I may feel worse than I already do"). Thus, every time I resist evil I am afraid. In order not "to resist evil" I must become courageous; in order to accept, I must be courageous. Courage does not mean foolhardiness. To be brave does not mean that I ignore fear or suppose it to be non-existent. To be brave means knowing how to cope with fear. This is to cultivate respect for that which, if feared without insight, would only grow more fearful. Courage is shown in two ways - endurance and action. The brave person endures and is durable, but he is not passive. He goes into action, on his own time, in his own way and most of the time on his own self. But his courage is pointless in itself.

Courage here is for the sake of something else - the ideas which make him what he is. Actually to face danger or evil is to contact it and to learn how to endure it, accept it and savor its meaning. Action is indicated in this experience. Though every brave act is also a patient one, passive suffering is not a lasting feature of endurance.

There comes the moment of action when suffering points the way to a creative experience, an act that gives meaning to the suffering and the evil endured. To contact evil is an essential quality of the courage to be!

Because academic man likes to classify, we now have a long list of types of disturbed people. There is an advantage to this. On the other hand, the classifying of types has given most people an unrealistic view of feeling problems. It has made it difficult to see at first hand that all personal problems have many factors in common. Then, too, in a group-therapy situation, it makes people tend to sit back, be restless, and wait for "their" type of problem to be discussed. The truth is all personal disorders have more in common that we will ever realize. To provide a simple easily understood basis for all personal problems - alcoholic, addictive, dependent, over-expectant or withdrawn - we can say that the common denominator is isolation, or the tendency towards it in various forms and attitudes. Isolation is the opposite of interpersonal health. Autism is the name given to the inner dependency of those feelings and values within the person who is moving toward isolation. Because empathy is the key action of good interpersonal health, autism is the key action of personal ill health.

What is it to be autistic? It is to retreat into a world of my own where my feelings about you and my values about the whole outside world are governed by old habitual fears and needs. My love for you may be mixed with fear of a strong dependence, if you are a woman who is like my mother. I can be hostile towards you if you do not behave in a way to suit me. I can also over-idealize you, making more of you than I should, because I expect too much of you for my sake, unable to allow you to be a person in your own right. Fantasies, hallucinations and delusions can arise in deep withdrawal as I make myself more and more inaccessible to you. You, other people and countless life situations then cease to be what they really are and become what I make of them in my isolated daydreaming. In this way I could go on indefinitely afraid of women and liking them too, in a bizarre love-hate pattern, governed by the trend of old fears and needs, if I did not know how to be free. To be autistic is to be a wishful thinker. To think wishfully is to be governed by desires and needs that are not beneficial to me because wishes can be riddled by fear as by love or joy. When I am autistic I therefore get a distorted picture of you and everything else. My opinion of you is not based on what you actually are, kind, personable, and humorous. I may feel that you are calculating, threatening and ridiculing. I am steeped in wishful thinking. As bad as that, I may also have a distorted, inadequate self image, abusing myself with guilt and depressed feelings and loneliness that are in fact unnecessary and unavoidable.

To be autistic means that I am unable to put myself in your place because I am isolated by my defenses against you and the whole world. My defenses mean essentially that my relation to you and to the world is a pattern of fear. Everything I feel and do is designed to protect and preserve myself against possible harm. The irony of it all is that I lose myself, I lose my personal meaning in the practice of such fear.